The Book

Ten reindeer does hurry toward the northern Alaskan tundra where their baby calves can be born in safety. They will journey over 500 miles, following ancient migratory routes traveled by their ancestors.

The new-born calves will spend a relaxed summer with their mothers learning to become a part of the herd. But this year when the animals move south to winter, they will face a new menace—the oil pipeline which cuts across their routes.

Alice L. Hopf traces the life cycle of an American reindeer, known as a caribou, through its first year. The young calf experiences many dangers—a grizzly bear, swift-flowing, icy rivers which must be crossed, hunter's guns, and harsh winter storms.

John Groth's striking illustrations provide a dramatic and realistic look at this American animal that has survived from the Ice Age.

BIOGRAPHY OF AN
American Reindeer

by Alice L. Hopf
paintings by John Groth

G. P. Putnam's Sons New York

Text copyright © 1976 by Alice L. Hopf
Illustrations copyright © 1976 by John Groth
All rights reserved. Published simultaneously in
Canada by Longman Canada Limited, Toronto.
PRINTED IN THE UNITED STATES OF AMERICA
07210
Library of Congress Cataloging in Publication Data
Hopf, Alice Lightner, 1904-
Biography of an American reindeer.
(Nature biography series)
SUMMARY: Portrays the life cycle of American
reindeer living in the Arctic.
1. Reindeer—Juvenile Literature. [1. Reindeer]
I. Groth, John, 1908-   II. Title.
QL737.U55H67 1976   599'.7357   76-5497
ISBN 0-399-20519-5
ISBN 0-399-61009-X lib. bdg.

For Michele

BIOGRAPHY OF AN
American Reindeer

The mother reindeer was hurrying. Spring
was coming, and her baby would soon be born.
Along with ten other does, she was headed for
the calving grounds on the northern Alaskan

tundra where the rich grass and lichen grow. There her fawn would be born in safe surroundings.

All the does were carrying unborn fawns. They had come a long way, almost five hundred miles. They were thin, and their ribs and hipbones stuck out. Their coats were worn and bleached. But their udders hung down, full of milk for the fawns that would soon be born.

Reindeer live on all the lands around the North Pole. In Alaska and Canada they are called caribou. In Europe and Asia they are known as reindeer. But they are all the same animal, and scientists call them *Rangifer tarandus*.

Reindeer lived as long ago as the great Ice Ages. Most of the animals that thrived then, such as the mammoth, the woolly rhinoceros, and the great cave bear, are now extinct. But the reindeer has survived. There are about thirteen separate herds living in Alaska today.

Because the reindeer, or caribou, is an Ice Age animal, it can only live in the north where it is cold. It has a thick, woolly coat. Even its nose is covered with fur. Over most of its body it has long guard hairs that are hollow. These hairs are filled with air so that when a caribou swims, the hairs serve as a kind of life jacket to help keep the animal from sinking.

The caribou has large, splayed feet that act as snowshoes. They help the caribou walk on the snow in winter and over boggy tundra in summer. The bones in their feet sometimes make an odd clicking noise as they walk.

Both the bucks (the males) and the does have

antlers, which begin to grow in the spring and are not fully grown until fall. In all other species of deer, only the bucks have antlers.

The lead doe climbed up a ridge and made her way along the top, where the wind had blown most of the snow away. She scratched off the thin covering to get at the green plants underneath. The other does followed her. They nibbled a mouthful here and a bit there, but they did not delay their journey north.

Their path led down off the ridge and across the snow-covered tundra. As the last doe stepped down onto the treeless plain that stretches like a white, unending sheet to the north, two wolves appeared, noses to the trail. The doe sprinted to catch up with the other caribou. The wolves began to race after them. The caribou put

on speed. In a few minutes they had left the wolves far behind. The wolves gave up the chase and began to look for something else to eat.

The mother caribou pressed on. In places the trail had been worn down by caribou traveling the same route year after year. The does could follow the trail easily.

The north country has many large rivers, such as the Yukon and the Porcupine. When the mother caribou came to a wide river, she plunged right in and swam strongly toward the far shore. The other does swam after her. Their heavy fur protected them from the icy water, and the guard hairs helped them stay afloat.

When they reached the other side, one of the does began to lag behind. The others slowed as though waiting for her to catch up. But the doe began to walk in circles. She raised and lowered her head, and she seemed frightened. Soon the legs of a baby fawn appeared, and in a few minutes a newborn fawn was lying on the snowy

ground. The mother licked it all over and poked it with her nose, urging it to get up. It fell down again, and the mother licked it some more.

The other caribou waited, but as soon as the baby was on its feet, the lead doe started north again. The others followed. The newborn fawn tried to follow but soon fell down. Its mother stood over it and licked it. After several efforts it managed to stay on its feet and follow its mother.

Two days later the does reached the shore of a wide river. The lead doe plunged in and began the long swim across. The doe and her little fawn were the last to enter the river. The baby stood on the shore and bawled while the mother urged it into the water. She came back several times and nuzzled it. At last the little fawn stepped into the cold water and started to swim. The mother deer stayed close to it, nudging it along with her bobbing head.

In the middle of the river the current was strong. The little fawn was tired. It could not keep going. It was carried away from its mother and swept down the river, crying weakly. The mother deer scrambled out of the river and ran along the bank. She called and called to her baby, but there was no answer. She stood with her head low and stared at the swift-moving water.

At last the mother deer saw that the others had gone on, and she followed after them. She would have no fawn to care for when they reached the calving grounds. Almost half the newborn caribou fawns die for one reason or another before they are a year old.

None of the other does gave birth to their fawns until they arrived at the calving grounds in the hilly country near the Arctic Ocean. Here the weather was colder, and there were fewer blackflies and mosquitoes to bite them.

Spring was coming. The ice was breaking up along the shore and in the rivers. The snow was melting, and green plants and flowers were pushing through the snow. Millions of birds were arriving to build their nests and raise their young. Mice and lemmings, wolves and foxes, weasels and hares had nests and dens full of wriggling babies.

A few days after they arrived, the lead doe gave birth to her baby fawn in a snowdrift. She licked him dry and nudged him onto his feet. Soon he was drinking his first meal from her milk-filled udder.

The rich milk helped the fawn grow fast. On his second day he could run after his mother. By the third day he could run just as fast as she did. Within ten days he had doubled his birth weight of thirteen pounds.

The summer sun blazed down both day and night in this northern land where there are twenty-four hours of daylight in the peak of summer and none in the middle of winter. The snow was melting faster every day, and plants and flowers were sprouting hourly from the tundra.

The mother doe wandered slowly from place to place, picking out the best plants to eat. The little fawn stayed close beside her. She nipped off the new, delicate shoots, leaving the rest of the plant, which could go on growing. She ate bog laurel and sedges, wintergreen and cranberry.

But she would not touch heath or the globe-flower or the needles of pine trees. Caribou are fussy eaters.

More and more does arrived at the calving grounds. Here they no longer stayed in large groups. They spread out in groups of twos and

threes, all looking for their favorite foods.

The fawn's mother liked to wander along the seashore, where she found strands of seaweed among the debris washed up by the Arctic waves. She liked the salty taste of these algae. Sometimes she found a dead fish among the seaweed or on the sand.

Caribou crave salt. During the long winter months they get their drinking water from snow, which does not have any salt. While caribou are considered plant-eating animals, they will occasionally eat fish and even meat for its salt.

The fawn followed his mother everywhere. He watched what she ate. Now and then he took a bite of a tender plant, but mostly he lived on her rich milk.

Soon he was playing with the other fawns on the tundra. They ran back and forth between their grazing mothers. They jumped in the air. They grew larger and faster every day. Sometimes they chased and butted each other. In four weeks little antler spikes began to sprout on their heads.

Other creatures shared the summer tundra with the caribou. The little fawn discovered this

when he was chasing another fawn. Suddenly a
hen ptarmigan flew up in front of his feet, and
the fawn shied away in fright. The mother bird
had waited until the last minute to leave her
nest. If the fawn had not shied away, her eggs
would have been crushed by his sharp hooves.

Another time, as he sniffed curiously at a hole in the tundra, another little nose poked out and sniffed him. The two baby animals stared at each other in surprise. Then the little fox snarled, and the fawn leaped into the air and ran off. If the mother fox had been in the den, the fawn's life might have ended right there. He ran back to his mother. He was learning that it was safer to stay near her and the other caribou.

During the short Arctic summer the young animals grow fast. By the time the fawn was half grown, he was out of much danger. Only wolves or bears were a serious threat, and they seldom appeared.

Now more and more caribou joined the does. These were the bucks that came north later than the does. The little fawn looked curiously at the great animals. They were larger than his mother,

and they had much bigger antlers. At first the
fawn was afraid. He ran to his mother for protection. But soon he grew used to the big males and
frisked around them, keeping just out of reach
of their hooves and antlers.

The bucks were often short-tempered. In the height of summer the mosquitoes and blackflies swarm here by the Arctic Ocean. They gathered on the caribou and bit them constantly. The animals would rush into the cold streams to get

away from their tormentors. At first the water felt very cold to the fawn, but he soon got used to it. It prepared him for the cold rivers and lakes he would have to swim across on the way south in the fall.

One day a new animal appeared near the herd
—a large, brown, furry animal. The fawn stared
at it in surprise. But his mother ran away,
bobbing her head for him to follow. All the
caribou ran, and the brown bear ran after them.
It was gaining on the fawn when a buck stepped
between them. The buck lowered his head with

the antlers pointing at the bear. His hind legs were spread in the fighting stance. He snorted at the bear. The bear stopped. He looked at the big rack of sharp antlers. He quickly lost interest in the fawn and ambled off in another direction. The fawn was glad to catch up with his mother.

In the days that followed, the fawn noticed
little furry animals running through the tundra
grass. At first he saw only a few. But soon they
seemed to be everywhere. When he almost
stepped on them, they shot out from under his
hooves, making him jump aside and shy wildly.

The little caribou put his nose down to get a better look. But they squeaked at him and ran away so fast that he couldn't follow them. While he was chasing one, another would pop up in front of him.

They were lemmings, small rodents that live in the Arctic. They have short tails and furry feet. Some years there are so many that they journey south in huge swarms, swimming across lakes and rivers and even jumping off cliffs into the ocean.

This was a good summer for lemmings. They were everywhere, running back and forth through the grass. Soon all the caribou were jumping and shying and chasing the lemmings. Then the fawn noticed that his mother was not chasing them just for fun. When she caught one, she ate it. Scientists believe that when a lemming is caught, it urinates in fear, and this supplies the salt the caribou crave.

The sun no longer stayed above the horizon all the time, and the summer days grew shorter and shorter. Twilight became longer, and soon there were even short periods of night.

Birds and animals that cannot live in the Arctic winter prepared to migrate, or journey, south. Great flocks of ducks and geese took off. Other birds followed.

The ptarmigan, which would stay in the north all winter, began to shed its brown feathers. Little by little they were replaced with white ones. By the time the snow fell it would be an all-white bird, almost invisible in the snow. Weasels and foxes also take on beautiful all-white coats in the Arctic during the winter.

Some animals prepare for winter by eating

until they are very fat and then going to sleep in a deep burrow or cave. The brown bear was one of these. All summer he had stuffed himself on vegetables, fish, and any meat he could catch. In later summer he gobbled blueberries, cranberries, and other fruits. When winter came, he would find a safe den, where he would sleep under a blanket of snow until spring.

But caribou cannot hibernate like the bear. The deep Arctic snow makes it impossible for them to find food in winter. They have to migrate south to the forest regions. There the trees protect them against the fierce winter winds, and they can find enough vegetation to eat.

Before the first flurries of snow the caribou began their migration. The fawn's mother and the other does in her group were among the first to go. The fawns followed them. Soon they were

moving at a steady pace, pausing only now and
then to eat.

Other herds of caribou joined them. Bucks
and does came from all directions, pouring down
into the migration route that has been used for

centuries to lead them to the winter range.
Streams of caribou flowed together in one huge
river of animals. Behind, in front, and along the
edges, sentinel animals watched for danger and
hurried stragglers if wolves appeared.

The caribou came to a blue lake. The leaders walked in and swam. All the caribou followed. If one animal hesitated, it was pushed into the water by those from behind.

The little fawn swam strongly beside his mother. The lake water was cold, but he was used to that. It was a sunny day, and the water was not rough.

A few days later they came to a wide river. It was not as long a swim as across the lake, but there was a swift current. The fawn was separated from his mother. He kept swimming until he staggered out on the other side. Some of the young fawns were not so lucky. They were swept downstream and drowned. The fawn stood on the beach and howled until his mother found him.

The migration went on. It looked like a sea of moving antlers. If a wolf pulled down a caribou along the edge of the herd, the other caribou just kept going. They crossed the tundra and the mountains, the rivers and the lakes. It seemed that nothing could stop the huge herd as it hurried south.

Then, one day, the herd came to a barrier that was new to them. The leaders stopped. They had

39

never seen anything like this before. Directly across their migration route curled a long black object. It was about as high as the lead buck's nose. He eyed it warily, watching to see if it did anything to threaten him.

The big buck could not know that this was a model of the great pipeline that would carry oil from the shores of the Arctic Ocean. The line would cross Alaska from north to south. It would crisscross the migration routes of the caribou herds in several places. What would the caribou do when the pipeline blocked their path? Concerned scientists were trying to find out. They had made this model and set it up before the caribou arrived. They had designed two gravel ramps where the caribou could cross over the pipe and four underpasses so that they could go under it.

The big buck stood still and watched the pipeline out of the corner of his eye. Nothing happened, but he did not trust it. There was a human smell about it which he did not like.

Suddenly the buck reared up on his hind legs and snorted loudly. His white mane blew in the wind. He pranced on his hind legs for several steps, then whirled and raced off, away from the thing that had frightened him. Most of the great herd followed.

Some of the caribou were pressed from behind and pushed to the side. When this happened near a ramp or an underpass, they crossed the pipeline.

The fawn's mother was well back in the herd. She was pushed to the side, and when she saw an underpass in front of her, she ran through it. Then she began looking for her fawn. She ran up and down the barrier, calling.

Finally, the fawn heard her and bleated back from his side. The top of his head was about level with the pipe, so he bent down and ducked under it. He ran to his mother, and she nuzzled him. Then they hurried to catch up with the small herd of caribou that had crossed the barrier.

Most of the herd that had refused to use the ramps and underpasses would have to find a new winter range. They could not be sure where their wanderings would take them. What would happen to other herds when the pipeline was built all the way across Alaska? The future of the caribou was in doubt.

The small herd which the mother caribou and her fawn had joined continued their usual journey south.

One day they came to a pass through the

mountains. The lead buck stopped and sniffed the air. He smelled danger on the wind, but he did not know where it came from. This was the first time he had led the herd because the older experienced bucks had left them at the pipeline.

Suddenly the buck bolted and dashed through the pass. He left an odor of fright where he had stood. The other caribou smelled it and ran after him. A few panicked and ran back. Guns blazed from the sides of the pass. The noise frightened the caribou more than ever. Three of them fell and lay dead on the tundra.

When the caribou had gone, a group of Eskimos came out of hiding. "Only three?" they said. "Where is the rest of the herd? Why are there so few this year? Three caribou will not feed all our village for the winter."

The little fawn and his mother had escaped with the herd. Finally, the caribou settled down again to a steady pace. The lead deer stayed alert for danger. They all sniffed the wind and listened for every sound. They stayed in open places, where they could see all around.

At last the herd came to the first trees they had seen on their journey south. They went on until they found a thick forest of trees and walked along its edge. They had been traveling for several weeks. They did not need to hurry now. They would winter here where the dense forest would protect them from the worst storms and where they could find food.

The herd wandered in the edges of the forest. They nibbled on tree lichen hanging down from the branches. Mushrooms and other woodland fungi were among their favorite foods that grew here. They looked for them carefully and quickly ate any they found.

Sometimes caribou eat toadstools which can be poisonous to human beings. But the caribou are tough animals, and the poisonous toadstools only make them sleepy. After eating some, a caribou will stand in a daze, forgetting what it was doing. When this happens, the animal is an easy target for a predator. But the caribou usually recovers before anything happens.

At this time of year the bucks have many-

47

pronged antlers on their large heads. The does have smaller antlers. Even the fawns have grown two small spikes on their heads.

In the forest the caribou began rubbing their antlers against the trees. The "velvet," the outside skin of the antler, was falling off. They rubbed and scraped to get it all off. The antlers became bare bones with sharp points. The bucks rubbed the most. They wanted to make their antlers as sharp as possible. They were good weapons, and the time of battles to determine the strongest bucks in the herd was coming.

This year the situation was unusual. The strongest bucks, who had been the leaders for several years, had stayed on the other side of the pipeline. This left many young bucks of two and three years of age in this smaller herd. They began to compete for position in the herd, and not a day passed without a duel of strength.

The bucks put their heads down and ran to-

gether. There was a great clashing of antlers and
much snorting and roaring. They pushed and
pushed, each trying to force the other backward
or down to the ground in an effort to drive the
other away. Some of the bucks were cut and
stabbed by the sharp spikes.

51

Finally, two or three of the strongest bucks were able to drive the others away. Each of these bucks collected a group of does and herded them off. The fawn's mother went with the strongest buck. They stayed together in a group. The buck mated with each doe. Because he was a strong buck, his offspring would be strong when they were born in the spring.

The fawn was frightened by all the fighting. He was separated from his mother. He was afraid of the snorting and pushing and clashing. This was no longer play, such as he and the other young caribou had enjoyed on the tundra. He ran off with a group of young males, and they stayed together and out of the way during the mating season.

As fall turned to winter, the trees shed their

leaves. Only the fir trees remained green. The bucks now began shedding their antlers completely. The little fawn's would fall off, too, but this would happen later in the year.

Now winter closed down on the northern lands. It was a time of cold and darkness. The days grew even shorter until the sun no longer rose above the horizon. Snow and wind brought fierce blizzards. The caribou moved into the forest for protection. The bucks wandered farther in, but the does stayed near the edge of the trees.

Winter is not a hardship for the caribou because they know how to live in snow. The fawn watched his mother and the other caribou. He learned how to dig for food under the snow. When he saw a few dry stems sticking out of a snowdrift, he knew that there would be fresh

green shoots farther down. He dug with his sharp hooves. He found wintergreen and cranberry and even marsh grass. When the snow was too deep for digging, he left his mother and followed the bucks even deeper into the forest. He ate the twigs of black spruce and other evergreens and the lichens that grew on the trees.

At last winter passed, and the sun returned to the northern lands. The days got longer. Snow began to melt, and there were signs of spring everywhere.

Now the does began to act nervous. It was time for them to migrate north to the calving grounds. In a few months their fawns would be born, and they had five hundred miles to travel.

The fawn was now a young buck, and he and the other young males stayed with the older bucks. When they moved back to the edge of the forest from deep in the woods, the females had already started north. But the young buck didn't need his mother anymore. He could take care of himself, and he would stay with the other males.

The young males followed the older bucks and did what they did. When the leaders went

north, they followed. The young buck watched the big bucks as they stood on guard as sentries. He learned how to be alert to danger and where to find the best food. And he learned about the migration northward. By sight and smell, he would remember the route. In a few years, when it was his turn to lead the herd, he would be ready.

The Author

ALICE L. HOPF is equally at home writing science fiction (under her maiden name, A. M. Lightner) and writing about nature. She is a member of the Lepidoterists Society, the New York Entomological Society, and the Audubon Society. She has written several other nature and animals books for Putnam's, including *Butterfly and Moth, Carab the Trap-Door Spider, Biography of an Octopus, Biography of a Rhino, Biography of an Armadillo, Wild Cousins of the Dog,* and *Wild Cousins of the Cat.*

The Artist

JOHN GROTH was born in Chicago and attended the School of the Chicago Art Institute. He also studied at the Royal Academy of London and the Arts Students League of New York. His drawings and paintings have been exhibited in major galleries and museums and in the permanent collection of the Metropolitan Museum of Art, the Museum of Modern Art, the Chicago Art Institute, the Brooklyn Museum, and the Smithsonian Institution.